D1212780

by Susan Kesselring • illustrated by Susan DeSantis

Published by The Child's World®
1980 Lookout Drive • Mankato, MN 56003-1705
800-599-READ • www.childsworld.com

ACKNOWLEDGMENTS
The Child's World®: Mary Berendes, Publishing Director
The Design Lab: Design and production
Red Line Editorial: Editorial direction

ISBN: 978-1-60973-200-4
LCCN: 2011927709

Printed in the United States of America
Mankato, MN
July 2011
PA02088

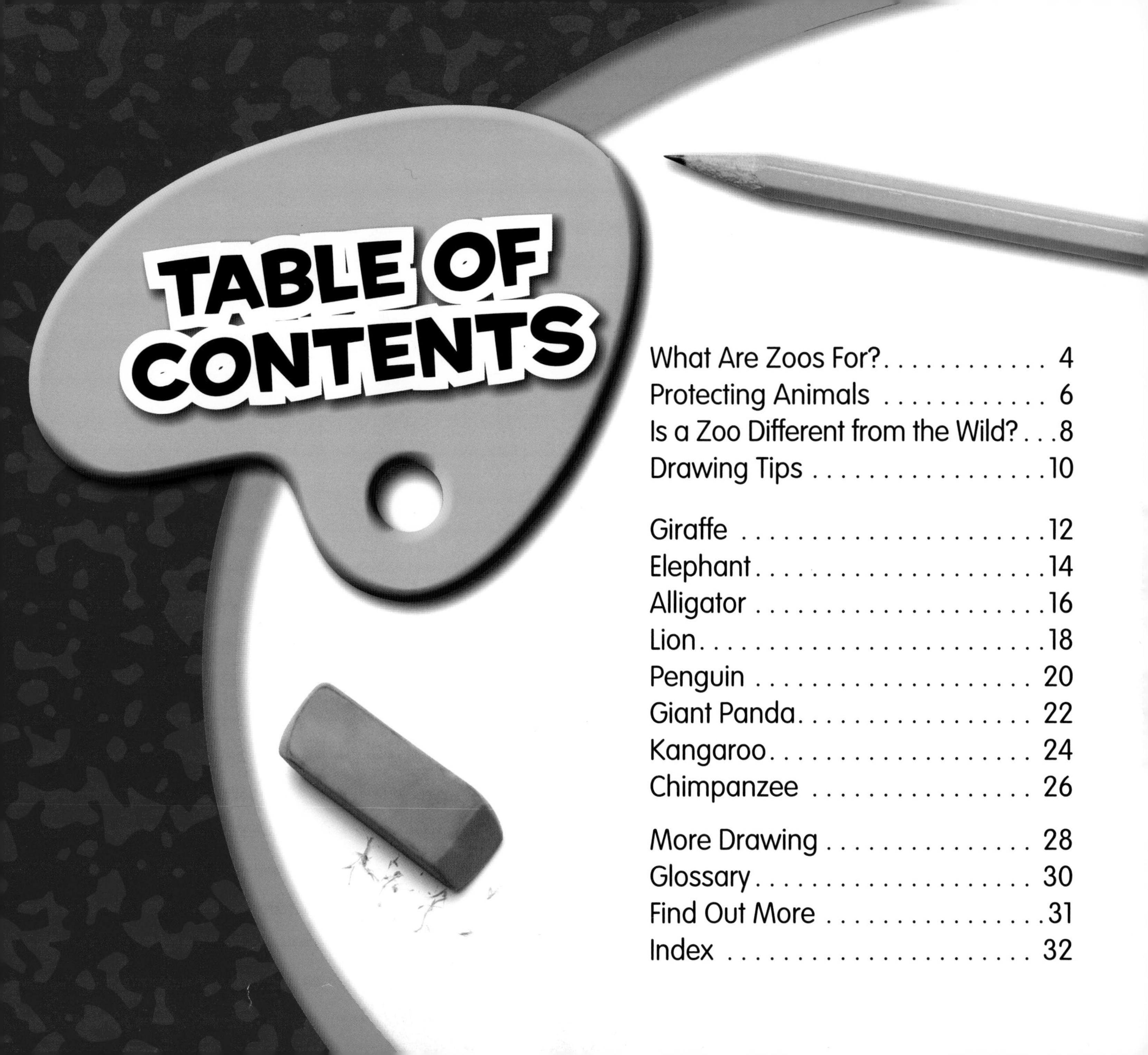

TABLE OF CONTENTS

WHAT ARE ZOOS FOR?

In the 1800s, American explorers traveled to faraway lands. They saw many different kinds of animals. People in the United States wanted to see these animals, too. Some people built a zoo for this reason. The Philadelphia Zoo opened in 1874. It was the first zoo in the United States. Today, people still like to see zoo animals.

But zoos do more than show off animals. People who work at zoos study the animals. They learn more about their eating habits. They learn how to keep the animals healthy. Zoos also teach visitors about the animals. Zoos have special programs that teach people about seals, lions, and more.

Zoos also protect animals. Some animals are in danger of dying out. There are only a few left in the wild. Zoos keep these animals safe. Their babies are protected, too. Giant pandas are often raised in zoos. There are only about 1,000 giant pandas left in the wild. It is important that some are raised in zoos so they don't die out.

Zookeepers teach people how important it is to save these animals and their **habitats**. They think that people will want to help animals if they understand them better.

IS A ZOO DIFFERENT FROM THE WILD?

Living in a zoo is different from living in the wild. In a zoo, the animal has good food and medicine. It is free from danger from **predators**. But it is not free to roam and to hunt for its food like it could in the wild. Crowds of people and lots of noise make zoo life very different.

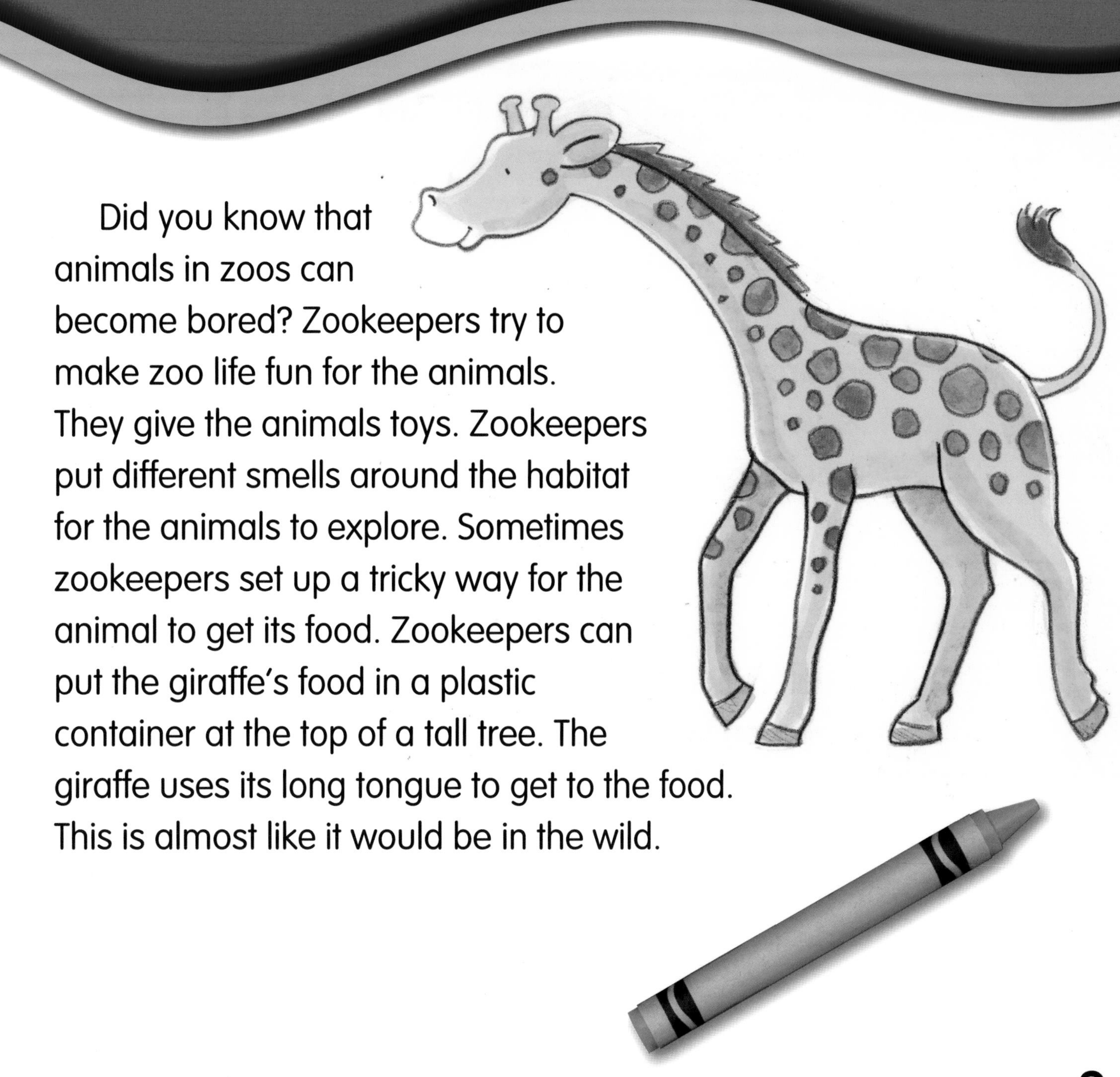

Did you know that animals in zoos can become bored? Zookeepers try to make zoo life fun for the animals. They give the animals toys. Zookeepers put different smells around the habitat for the animals to explore. Sometimes zookeepers set up a tricky way for the animal to get its food. Zookeepers can put the giraffe's food in a plastic container at the top of a tall tree. The giraffe uses its long tongue to get to the food. This is almost like it would be in the wild.

DRAWING TIPS

You've learned about zoo animals. You're almost ready to draw them. But first, here are a few drawing tips:

Every artist needs tools. To learn how to draw zoo animals, you will need:

- Some paper
- A pencil
- An eraser
- Markers, crayons, colored pencils, or watercolors (optional)

Anyone can learn to draw. You might think only some people can draw. That's not true. Everyone can learn to draw. It takes practice, though. The more you draw, the better you will be. With practice, you will become a true artist!

Everyone makes mistakes. This is okay! Mistakes help you learn. They help you know what not to do next time. Mistakes can even make your drawing more special. It's all right if you draw the elephant's ears too big. Now you've got a one-of-a-kind drawing. You can erase a mistake you don't like, too. Then start again!

Stay loose. Relax your body before you begin. Hold your pencil lightly. Don't rest your wrist on the table. Instead, move your whole arm as you draw. This will help you make smooth lines. Press lightly on the paper when you draw or erase.

Drawing is fun! The most important thing about drawing is to have fun. Be creative. Your drawings don't have to look exactly like the pictures in this book. Try making the penguin smaller or the elephant really big. You can also use markers, crayons, colored pencils, or watercolors to bring your zoo animals to life.

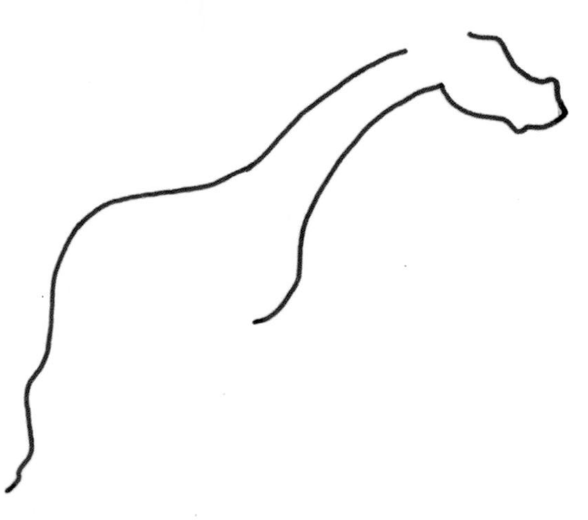

GIRAFFE

The giraffe is the tallest animal in the world. It can stand 19 feet (5.8 m) tall. It can reach the leaves at the tops of trees that other animals can't reach.

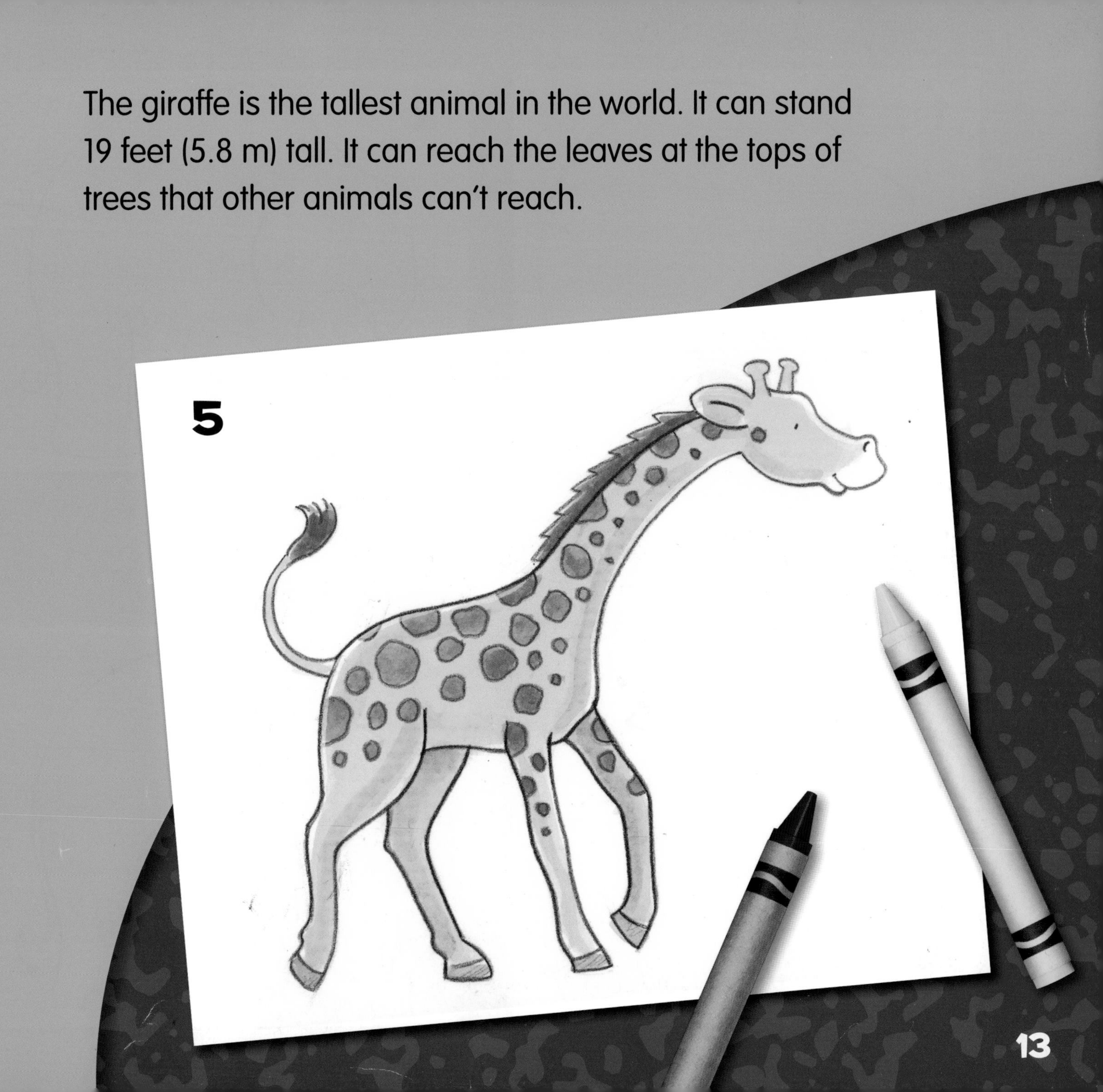

ELEPHANT

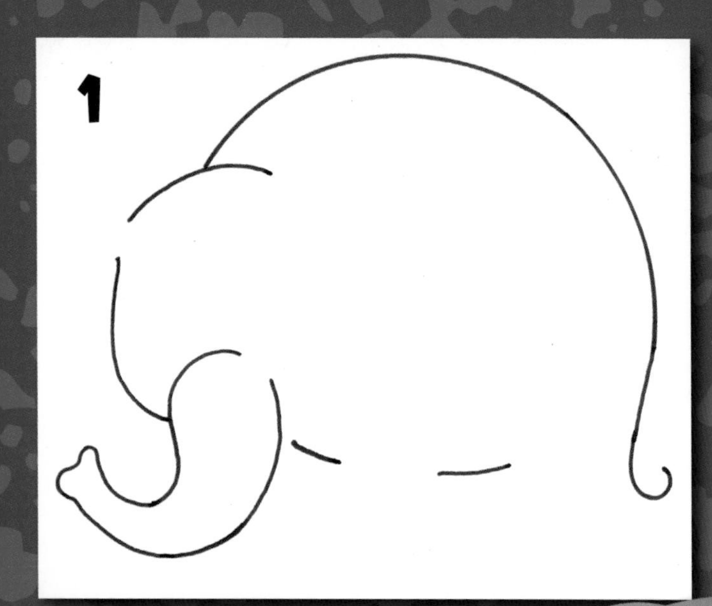

An elephant's trunk has many uses. It is a nose. It scoops up drinking water, too. The trunk is also a snorkel in deep water, a warning trumpet, or an arm for hugging.

ALLIGATOR

1

2

3

4

An alligator looks like a giant lizard. It is a great swimmer. It uses its long, strong tail and webbed feet to move through the water.

LION

The male lion is known for the long, shaggy mane around its head and neck. Some people think the mane protects the lion's throat during a fight.

PENGUIN

1

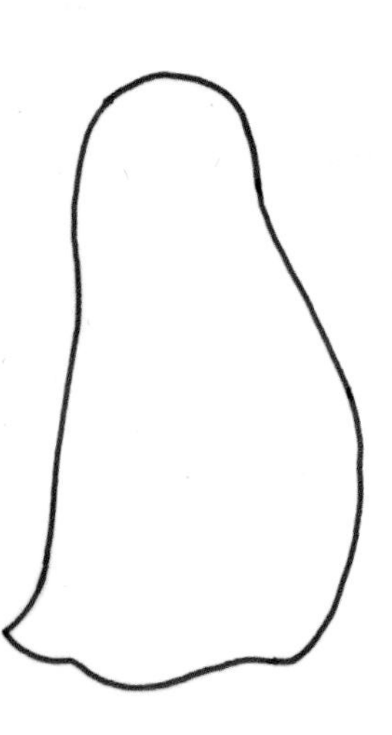

2

3

4

There are 17 **species** of penguins in the world. The emperor penguin is the largest. It stands a little less than 4 feet (1.2 m) tall.

GIANT PANDA

Giant pandas mainly eat **bamboo**. This is a type of plant. They can eat up to 40 pounds (18 kg) a day. That's a lot of bamboo!

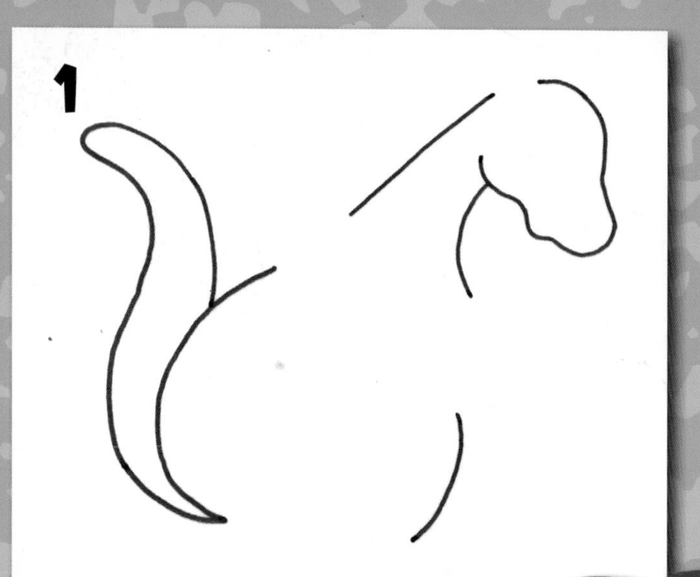

KANGAROO

The kangaroo hops everywhere it goes. It can jump 25 feet (7.6 m) in a single hop. A baby kangaroo is a **joey**. A joey rides in its mother's pouch.

CHIMPANZEE

1

2

3

4

A chimpanzee looks a lot like a human. It mostly walks on all four legs. But it can walk on its back legs for short distances.

MORE DRAWING

Now you know how to draw zoo animals. Here are some ways to keep drawing them.

Zoo animals come in all different colors, shapes, sizes, and textures. You can draw them all! Try using pens or colored pencils to draw and color in details. Experiment with crayons and markers to give your drawings different colors and textures. You can also paint your drawings. Watercolors are easy to use. If you make a mistake, you can wipe it away with a damp cloth. Try tracing the outline of your drawing with a crayon or a marker. Then paint over it with watercolor. What happens?

Drawing Field Trip

When you want something new to draw, take a field trip. Visit a zoo! Find an animal that you haven't drawn before. Look at it carefully. Does it stand on two or four legs? Does it have a tail? Does it have paws, wings, or feathers? Now try drawing it! If you need help, use the examples in this book to guide you.

GLOSSARY

bamboo (bam-BOO): Bamboo is a plant with a hard, hollow stem. Pandas mainly eat bamboo.

habitats (HAB-uh-tats): Habitats are the places where animals or plants naturally live. Zoos teach visitors about animals' habitats.

joey (JO-ee): A joey is a baby kangaroo. A joey travels in its mother's pouch.

predators (PRED-uh-turs): Predators are animals that live by killing and eating other animals. Animals in zoos are safe from predators.

species (SPEE-sheez): A species is a group of animals or plants that is divided based on its characteristics. Elephants are one species.

zookeepers (ZOO-keep-urs): Zookeepers are people who take care of animals in a zoo. Zookeepers may help train the animals.

FIND OUT MORE

BOOKS

Emberley, Ed. *Ed Emberley's Drawing Book: Make a World*. New York: Little Brown, 2006.

Gravel, Elise. *Let's Draw and Doodle Together*. Maplewood, NJ: Blue Apple Books, 2010.

Winterberg, Jenna. *The Zoo: A Step-by-Step Drawing & Story Book*. Minneapolis, MN: Walter Foster, 2006.

WEB SITES

Visit our Web site for links about drawing zoo animals:

childsworld.com/links

Note to Parents, Teachers, and Librarians: We routinely verify our Web links to make sure they are safe and active sites. So encourage your readers to check them out!

ABOUT THE AUTHOR:

Susan Kesselring loves children, books, nature, and her family. She teaches K-1 students in a progressive charter school in Castle Rock, Minnesota.

ABOUT THE ILLUSTRATOR:

Susan DeSantis is a freelance children's book illustrator. She lives in Westerly, Rhode Island, with her husband and children. The art for this book was done in gouache and colored pencils on pressed watercolor paper.